T0112733

A Note from
Mary Pope Osborne About the

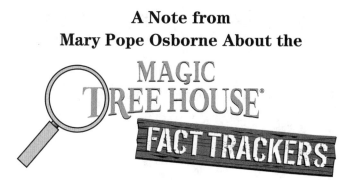

When I write Magic Tree House® adventures, I love including facts about the times and places Jack and Annie visit. But when readers finish these adventures, I want them to learn even more. So that's why we write a series of nonfiction books that are companions to the fiction titles in the Magic Tree House® series. We call these books Fact Trackers because we love to track the facts! Whether we're researching dinosaurs, pyramids, Pilgrims, sea monsters, or cobras, we're always amazed at how wondrous and surprising the real world is. We want you to experience the same wonder we do—so get out your pencils and notebooks and hit the trail with us. You can be a Magic Tree House® Fact Tracker, too!

Here's what kids, parents, and teachers have to say about the Magic Tree House® Fact Trackers:

"They are so good. I can't wait for the next one. All I can say for now is prepare to be amazed!" —Alexander N.

"I have read every Magic Tree House book there is. The [Fact Trackers] are a thrilling way to get more information about the special events in the story." —John R.

"These are fascinating nonfiction books that enhance the magical time-traveling adventures of Jack and Annie. I love these books, especially *American Revolution.* I was learning so much, and I didn't even know it!" —Tori Beth S.

"[They] are an excellent 'behind-the-scenes' look at what the [Magic Tree House fiction] has started in your imagination! You can't buy one without the other; they are such a complement to one another." —Erika N., mom

"Magic Tree House [Fact Trackers] took my children on a journey from Frog Creek, Pennsylvania, to so many significant historical events! The detailed manuals are a remarkable addition to the classic fiction Magic Tree House books we adore!" —Jenny S., mom

"[They] are very useful tools in my classroom, as they allow for students to be part of the planning process. Together, we find facts in the [Fact Trackers] to extend the learning introduced in the fictional companions. Researching and planning classroom activities, such as our class Olympics based on facts found in *Ancient Greece and the Olympics,* help create a genuine love for learning!" —Paula H., teacher

MAGIC TREE HOUSE®
FACT TRACKER

Sabertooths
and the Ice Age

A NONFICTION COMPANION TO MAGIC TREE HOUSE #7:
Sunset of the Sabertooth

BY MARY POPE OSBORNE
AND NATALIE POPE BOYCE

ILLUSTRATED BY SAL MURDOCCA

A STEPPING STONE BOOK™
Random House 🏠 New York

Text copyright © 2005 by Mary Pope Osborne and Natalie Pope Boyce
Interior illustrations copyright © 2005 by Sal Murdocca
Cover photograph courtesy of Mark Hallett Paleoart

The Magic Tree House Fact Tracker series was formerly known as the Magic Tree House
Research Guide series.

Visit us on the Web!
MagicTreeHouse.com
randomhousekids.com

Educators and librarians, for a variety of teaching tools, visit us at
RHTeachersLibrarians.com

Library of Congress Cataloging-in-Publication Data
Osborne, Mary Pope.
Sabertooths and the Ice Age : a nonfiction companion to Magic tree house #7,
sunset of the sabertooth / by Mary Pope Osborne and Natalie Pope Boyce ;
illustrated by Sal Murdocca.
   p.   cm. — (Magic tree house fact tracker)
"A Stepping Stone book."
ISBN 978-0-375-82380-0 (trade) — ISBN 978-0-375-92380-7 (lib. bdg.) —
ISBN 978-0-307-97530-0 (ebook)
1. Saber-toothed tigers—Juvenile literature. 2. Ice Age—Juvenile literature.
I. Title.
QE882.C15 O83 2011 569′.75—dc22   2011009362

Printed in the United States of America
32

This book has been officially leveled by using the F&P Text Level Gradient™
Leveling System.

For Bob and Mary Crowell

Historical Consultant:

DR. TOM ROTHWELL, Division of Paleontology, American Museum of Natural History, New York

Education Consultant:

HEIDI JOHNSON, Earth Science and Paleontology, Lowell Junior High School, Bisbee, Arizona

Very special thanks to Paul Coughlin for his great photographs; and to the wonderful collaborative team at Random House: Joanne Yates, Mallory Loehr, Diane Landolf, and, as always, our editor, Shana Corey, who once again encouraged and guided us every step of the way.

SABERTOOTHS
AND THE ICE AGE

Contents

Dear Readers,

When we finished our adventures in <u>Sunset of the Sabertooth</u>, we didn't want to leave the Ice Age. So we got out our pencils and paper to do some fact tracking.

We wanted to learn about the people of the Ice Age and the world of the saber-toothed cats. We started at the library. We searched the shelves for books we needed. Then we went to our computers to dig up more information. We found out so much about the lives of people thousands of years ago. Finally, we studied the big saber-toothed cats and other amazing animals.

We even read about animals frozen in ice and studied by scientists today!

So grab your notebooks and put on your warm coats. It's going to be a cold trip. We're leading you back into the Ice Age! Brrr!

Jack

Annie

1

The Ice Age

A million years ago, the world was much colder than it is now. Large parts of North America lay under ice and snow. Ice covered parts of Europe, Asia, and South America. In places it was a mile deep! We call this time the "Ice Age."

The Ice Age began long after the dinosaurs disappeared. It lasted thousands of years. It ended 10,000 years ago.

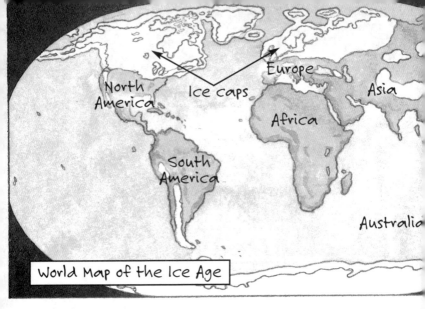

World Map of the Ice Age

During the Ice Age, the ocean froze between Britain and Greenland.

Whew! Some scientists believe we are in a warm phase of an ice age today.

The Ice Age was not one long period. In fact, scientists believe there have been several ice ages. At times the weather got warmer . . . warmer even than today. Years would pass, sometimes thousands of years. Then the temperatures slowly began to drop again. The icy weather returned.

What Causes Ice Ages

Scientists are not exactly sure why we have ice ages. But they do have an idea. They think Earth changes its orbit around the sun every 100,000 years.

Orbit means "the path one object takes around another."

During the Ice Age, Earth's orbit moved farther from the sun. Summers became too cold to melt ice and snow.

Brrr!

In some places, temperatures were 45 degrees colder than today.

Climate means "the weather in a place over a long period of time."

The Siberian land bridge was 55 miles long. In places it was 1,000 miles across.

Over millions of years, the warmer *climate* of the dinosaurs disappeared. The icy world of the saber-toothed cat took its place. Slowly the land itself began to change. Water froze into ice and was trapped on land. Ocean levels dropped.

As the water levels went down, land was exposed. A land bridge formed between England and France. Another appeared between Siberia and Alaska. People and animals used the bridges to cross from one place to another.

Glaciers

Many changes were caused by glaciers (GLAY-shurz). Glaciers are massive sheets of ice.

They form after many years of falling

snow. The snow piles up. It gets very heavy. Ice inside the piled-up snow melts. The melted snow freezes again. This time it forms into hard ice crystals.

Some ice crystals in a glacier are football-size!

Gravity begins to pull on the glacier. Slowly it begins to expand forward and sideways. Some glaciers can expand up to 1,000 feet a year. Others expand only a few inches.

In the Ice Age, glaciers acted like giant scrapers. As they expanded, they slowly cut through the land. They carried dirt along with them. Tons of rocks and sand were left behind. Lakes and valleys formed.

Rivers changed their paths. As the glaciers scraped the soil away, only scrubby bushes and grasses grew where large plants had once thrived.

Glaciers still exist today.

17

These boulders were left behind by a glacier in Alaska.

Ice Age

Earth's orbit changes

Temperatures drop

Ice covers parts of world

Ocean levels drop

Land bridges exposed

People and Animals

There were other changes in the Ice Age.

The first ancestors of modern humans appeared. Some lived in caves and wore skins and furs.

Ancestors are relatives who lived long ago.

Large animals that could survive the cold roamed the earth. Their bodies held in heat better than those of small animals.

Many Ice Age animals were *mammals* (MAM-ulz). Mammals have extra protection against harsh, freezing weather. They have hair for warmth. And they are warm-blooded. Their temperature doesn't change with the outside temperature. Mammals give birth to live babies. And mammal babies feed on their mothers' milk. Extra care by their mothers helps them survive.

People are mammals too.

What kinds of animals could live in this harsh world? And who were the people who lived in the caves of the Ice Age?

19

Glaciers Today

There is even a glacier in Africa . . . on Mount Kenya!

Today glaciers cover about 10 percent of the earth. The largest glaciers are in the Canadian Arctic, Antarctica, Alaska, the Andes Mountains in South America, and the Himalayan Mountains in Asia.

The smallest glaciers are the size of a sports field. They can also be more than 50 miles long! North America's longest

Glacier in New Zealand

glacier is in Alaska. It is called the Bering Glacier.

Glaciers can take as long as 3,000 years to form. When they get to be about 65 feet high, they begin to expand. Glaciers hold much of the freshwater in the world. If all the glaciers melted, ocean levels would rise.

When a glacier reaches the ocean, part of it breaks off. Then it becomes an iceberg.

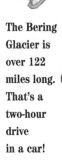

The Bering Glacier is over 122 miles long. That's a two-hour drive in a car!

Iceberg in Antarctica

2

![mammoth icon]

Early People
of the Ice Age

Some of the earliest Ice Age people were
the *Neanderthals* (nee-AN-dur-tallz).
Their *fossils* were first found in the
Neander Valley in Germany. Neander-
thals existed about 100,000 years ago.
They lived in Europe, the Middle East,
North Africa, and parts of Asia.

Fossils are
remains or
traces of life
from long
ago.

The fossils tell us that Neanderthals
were compact and muscular. They were

Neanderthals had wide noses to warm the icy air they breathed.

about five feet six inches tall and had thick bones.

Their heads bulged slightly in the back. Their foreheads jutted out over their eyes.

Neanderthals lived in caves or tents made of skins. They may have been the first people to wear clothes.

Scientists have found Neanderthal tools at Le Moustier (MOOSE-tee-ay), France. It was home to Neanderthals for thousands of years. They camped in the entrances to caves. They also lived under overhanging rocks. The tools found at this site are called the "Mousterian Tool Kit."

Chipping flint is called "flint napping."

The Neanderthals carefully chipped flakes from flint or other stone. The flakes were shaped into blades, knives, and scrapers.

24

Pointed tool

Scraper

Arrow

Scientists discovered 60 different kinds of flaked tools and 20 different kinds of small hand axes at Le Moustier.

The Old Man of Shanidar

Shanidar was home to a group of Neanderthals in Iraq. Scientists have discovered Neanderthal skeletons in a cave there. One skeleton has captured the scientists' imaginations. He is called the "Old Man of Shanidar."

Most Neanderthals died before they reached 35.

Actually, the "old man" was only 45 years old. That was very old in those days. He had lived a hard life. One arm was withered and useless. One of his eyes had been damaged. And he had head injuries.

And yet he was buried with care. A ring of stones surrounded his body. Someone had placed a bear's skull nearby. Scientists think the skull was part of a burial ceremony.

Scientists found pollen in the cave.

They tested the pollen to find what kind of flowers it produced. They discovered the same flowers growing near the cave today!

The flowers were hollyhocks, bachelor's buttons, and grape hyacinths.

We don't know much about the Neanderthals. We don't know anything about their language. Some scientists are not even sure they had a language. Because we have found tools, we know they were skillful toolmakers. Their remains tell us they lived in family groups. We also know they cared for their sick and old. And we are positive some even buried their dead. Neanderthals died out about 35,000 years ago. No one is certain exactly why.

Homo Sapiens

As time passed, other people slowly

Homo sapiens means "thinking man" in Latin.

replaced the Neanderthals. They were called *Homo sapiens* (HO-mo SAY-pee-unz). They are our early relatives. In fact, people today are still called "Homo sapiens."

Gradually these people spread out all over the world. Their remains have been found in Europe, Asia, Africa, and America.

Researchers believe many walked over the land bridge from Asia to North America. Some scientists think they even used small boats to reach the North American coast.

Homo sapiens began to cross over to North America about 13,000 years ago.

We have found tools and other remains at their campsites. These things tell us that Homo sapiens had more skills than Neanderthals. And they looked different. Their foreheads did not jut over their eyes. Their lower jaws did not push forward. Their faces were straighter. They

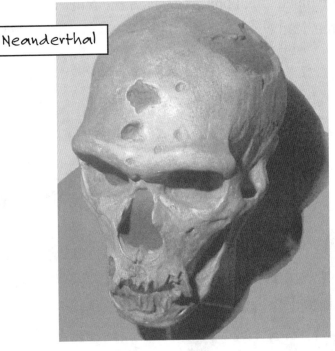

Neanderthal

had smaller noses and jaws. Their bones were lighter. They moved more freely.

Because they were so skillful, Homo sapiens were able to survive in harsh conditions. They hunted and gathered food. They built shelters and made warm clothes. Many were able to live very long lives.

An adult Homo sapiens male was about five feet six inches tall . . . as tall as Neanderthals.

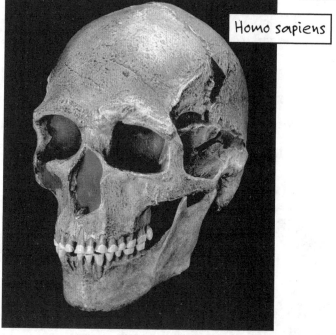

Homo sapiens

Fire!

Scientists aren't sure when people first started using fire. They do know that its use was one of the most important discoveries ever made.

Early people knew about fires caused by lightning strikes. But they didn't know how to make their own fire. They ate their food raw. They shivered in icy weather. And there was no light during the dark nights.

Finally, people figured out how to make fire. They rubbed two sticks together. The sticks grew warm. Soon a spark flew off. They found they could make sparks with stone as well. The sparks caught grass or wood on fire. When they made their own fires, they could stay warm. They could watch the flickering flames at night and have light.

Later they found out they could cook their food. (Maybe someone accidentally dropped some meat in the fire.) And best of all, fire scared away hungry animals that prowled in the night!

Warning!
Do not try to start fires like the Ice Age people did!

3

Life in the Ice Age

Russian scientists recently made an exciting discovery. They found a 30,000-year-old campsite! It was 300 miles north of the Arctic Circle. They discovered stone tools and ivory weapons at the site. And they also found piles of animal bones.

The campsite was used by a group of Homo sapiens called the *Cro-Magnon* (cro-MAG-nun). Cro-Magnon people lived

The first Cro-Magnon fossils were found in a cave called Cro-Magnon in France.

in Europe from 35,000 to 10,000 years ago. The Cro-Magnon looked a lot like we do. They were skillful toolmakers and hunters. They made their own clothes. They wove ropes, nets, and clothes from plant fibers. They even made musical instruments.

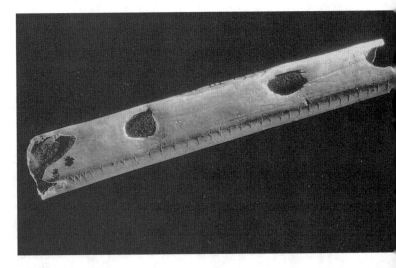

This Cro-Magnon flute was made from bird bone. It's 25,000 years old!

Houses

In the winter, Cro-Magnon people didn't move around much. Everyone lived in huts or longhouses made from mammoth bones, branches, and hides. When summer arrived, they left to follow the herds. Then they lived in tents made of animal hides. These were easy to move and set up.

Hunting

Ice Age campsites tell us Cro-Magnons were good hunters. They made weapons out of bone, ivory, antler, stone, and wood. They hunted with spears and knives. They also used bows and arrows.

Hunting could be difficult. Sometimes hunters tracked an animal for days. Sometimes they trapped animals in swamps. If an animal attacked, they had only simple weapons to defend themselves.

Ice Age people's skeletons showed many injuries.

Spearheads

When the hunters returned, there was much to do. Nothing was wasted. Animals

were not just for meat. Fur was peeled away from the hide. People used it for clothes or rugs to sleep and sit on. Hides were dried and stretched for clothes, tents, packs, and pouches.

Cro-Magnon people even saved the bones and the fat. Bones supported their tents or held up roofs. They used animal fat to burn in stone lamps. It gave them light on dark, cold nights.

Diet

Cro-Magnon people ate meat or fish whenever they could. Scientists think that reindeer provided much of their meat. When they killed an animal, they ate almost every part. They even ate the brains and livers and tongues!

Ice Age smoothie: For quick energy, people drank animal blood!

Cro-Magnons cooked over open fires.

Meat was often roasted on spits. Some-times it was boiled. The cooks put the meat into leather pouches. Then they heated water by dropping hot stones into pots.

Later they dried the leftover meat. They preserved it by rubbing salt into it. If it was icy, the ice acted like a freezer.

They also gathered plants, berries, eggs, nuts, and seeds. They picked dan-delions and all kinds of greens. They ate sunflower seeds and hazelnuts. They gathered plants or herbs like catnip for medicine.

Women and children usually did the gathering.

After they gathered the food, they car-ried it home in leather bags or pouches.

Clothing

People in the Ice Age needed warm clothes. In the winter, they wore clothes and shoes made of furs and animal skins. They also wore belts, cloaks, and warm hats. They sewed them together with needles made of bone or ivory.

This is a bone needle used for sewing.

Many researchers think Cro-Magnon people wove clothes from plant fibers. They wore these lighter clothes during the summer.

Burial

Cro-Magnons buried their dead in formal graves. Many skeletons have on beautiful bracelets and necklaces. They even have jewelry on their knees and elbows! The jewelry is made of shells, ivory, bone, and animal teeth.

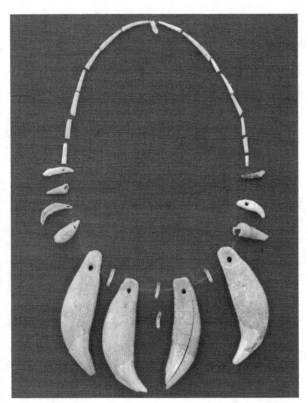

This necklace was found in France. It had teeth from bears, lions, wolves, deer, and foxes.

Three Cro-Magnon skeletons were found in Sungir, Russia. One was a 60-year-old man. The other two were a young boy and girl.

The man had about 3,000 ivory beads all over his body. He wore bracelets and a red necklace. The girl's and boy's bodies were each covered with about 5,000 beads! The boy wore a beaded cap decorated with fox teeth. He also wore a belt with 250 fox teeth. An ivory pin was at his throat.

When people today tried to carve beads like these, each bead took over an hour!

<u>Cro-Magnons</u>
Hunters and gatherers
Lived in tents, huts, caves
Good toolmakers
Formal burials

The Sungir graves show that Cro-Magnons honored their dead. They decorated the bodies of their dead friends and family. They probably performed ceremonies at the grave. They were the first people to perform burials like this.

Turn the page to learn about an Ice Age campsite.

Ice Age Campsite

Hides were stretched on a frame.

Researchers have found piles of flint chips from making tools.

Honey was the only sweet for children.
Early dogs came from wolves.
Bones held the pot up over the fire.
People piled stones around the fire to protect it from winds.

4

Cave Art

Recently scientists were searching Hohle Fels (HO-luh FELZ) Cave in Germany. Three small ivory objects caught their eye. They were figures of a horse, a bird, and a creature that was half human, half lion. They were carved over 30,000 years ago.

Ice Age people often carved animals and people out of ivory, bone, stone, and antlers. They also created figures out of clay.

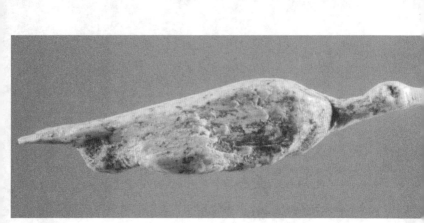

This waterbird carving was discovered at Hohle Fels Cave. It was carved from mammoth ivory.

Sometimes they painted wonderful pictures on cave walls. The artists walked deep into the pitch-black caves. Many caves were so narrow, they had to crawl on their stomachs. They lighted their way with torches of burning animal fat.

In one cave, they painted on a 20-foot-high ceiling!

Early artists usually painted animals

50

and hunters. Sometimes herds of animals decorated the walls. There were also human figures and handprints. Scientists do not believe the people actually lived in these caves. They think they were special caves for art.

Paint

Cave artists used minerals found in dirt as paint. The earliest paintings were mostly black. Later they added red to their paintings.

The red came from iron oxide buried in the ground. The artists dug up lumps of it and ground it into a paste. The red paint has lasted for thousands of years.

Artists painted with twigs and horse-hair brushes. They blended the paint with feathers. Sometimes they blew paint out of their mouths onto the walls! Sometimes they blew paint out of hollow animal horns.

The Cave of Lascaux

The dog's name was Robot.

One day in 1940, four French boys lost their puppy in the woods. They feared it had fallen down a deep hole. They lowered themselves down on ropes. To their surprise, they found themselves in a cave. What they saw there amazed them.

The cave walls were covered in drawings, paintings, and engravings. The boys saw herds of animals painted on the walls. There was a large bull and an upside-down horse.

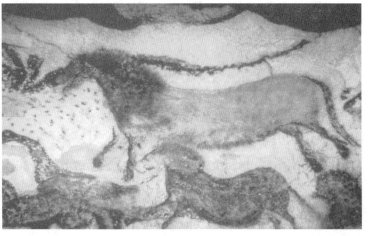

This painting of a herd of horses lasted so long because the cave was dry and dark.

They had found the cave of Lascaux (lass-KOH), one of the most important Ice Age sites in the world! Scientists date the art back to over 16,000 years ago.

People began to come from all over to see the incredible cave art. Experts worried that the paintings would be ruined.

Finally, the French government closed the cave. But it created a second cave nearby. It looks like the real one. Today visitors can only visit the new cave. The wonderful art of Lascaux remains safe, deep in its dark and magic cave.

Altamira

Altamira is a cave in Spain. In 1879, a young girl told her father about some strange cave paintings she'd heard about there.

Her father, Don Marcelino Sanz de Sautuola (mar-suh-LEE-no SAHNZ day sow-tu-OH-luh), had studied ancient cave art. He walked far back into the cave. What he saw startled him. The cave was covered in art. There were deer, wild boar, and bison. He was convinced the art was between 11,000 and 19,000 years old!

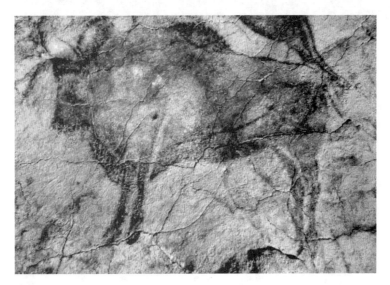

This bison is from the cave at Altamira.

People flocked to the cave. Then trouble began. Experts questioned Don Marcelino's conclusions. Some even thought the paintings were fake. They claimed his friends painted the pictures. When Don Marcelino died, people still doubted his discovery.

The king of Spain even visited.

Experts continued to study the cave.

56

Nearly 15 years after Don Marcelino's death, they all agreed he had been right.

Scientists found the remains of food in the cave. They also found tools and hearths for fire. Experts believe people actually lived there.

People have been creating art for thousands of years. Some scientists think early people made art to give them luck on the hunt. They may have done it to tell stories or create magic. But there are many experts who think these early artists just wanted to create something beautiful.

Turn the page to see our favorite cave paintings.

Jack and Annie's Gallery of Cave Art

Cave art often pictured animals of the hunt. Bison, horses, and bulls decorated many walls. Sometimes the artists painted hunters spearing game. They also showed hunters being injured. Some animal paintings were large. In Lascaux, there is a cow over five feet long, called the "leaping cow."

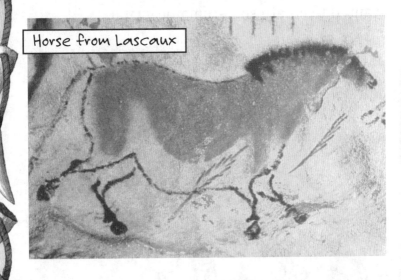

Horse from Lascaux

Hunting scene from Lascaux

Swimming stags from Lascaux

Here are some of our favorite cave paintings.

5

Saber-Toothed Cats in the Pits

Scientists don't just have clues about ancient humans. They have clues about animals too. Many animals of the Ice Age are extinct. *Extinct* means that the animals do not exist today. We only know about them from fossils.

One of the most famous fossil sites is right in downtown Los Angeles! This site is called the La Brea Tar Pits. The pits aren't actually tar pits. They are asphalt (AS-fault) pits. Asphalt is sticky and tar-like.

Asphalt comes from oil inside the earth. The oil leaks out to the surface. After many years, the oil turns into asphalt. And for 30,000 years, animals got stuck in it!

These animals got stuck in the asphalt by accident. Sometimes they were fleeing *predators*. When the predators spotted a struggling animal, they dashed in to get it. Then the predators also got

Bones from 34,000 large animals have been found in the pits.

Predators are animals that hunt and eat other animals.

stuck! Other times the animals mistook asphalt for water.

The La Brea Tar Pits became a burial ground for millions of plants, birds, insects, and animals. At least 2,500 saber-toothed cats are buried there. The La Brea site is the best place to study these fierce animals.

The La Brea pits hold 98 tons of fossils.

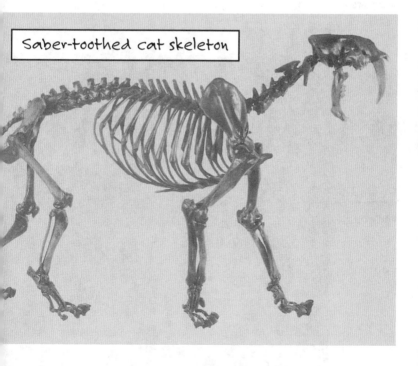

Saber-toothed cat skeleton

Saber-Toothed Cat

Sometimes saber-toothed cats are called saber-toothed tigers. They are not actually tigers. They belong to the cat family.

But you don't want a pet like this! Saber-toothed cats were some big, fierce cats! They get the name "saber-toothed" because their canine teeth were shaped like *sabers*.

A <u>saber</u> is a sharp sword.

<u>Smilodon</u> means "knife tooth."

These teeth were about nine inches long. Their upper teeth were also very sharp. They used these teeth to bite their victims' necks and bellies.

Scientists call the most common saber-toothed cat Smilodon (SMY-luh-don).

Saber-Toothed Cats on the Loose!

Saber-toothed cats were very danger-ous. They were meat eaters. They at-tacked anything that looked like dinner!

Scientists think they roared very loudly.

These cats were built to hunt. They were about three feet tall at their shoulders. Most were over six feet long. (This didn't include their short tails.) They weighed over 600 pounds.

Saber-toothed cats could probably run very fast. But they could only run for short distances. They used their powerful legs to kick out at their prey. Then they would whip out their sharp claws. These claws could be pulled in and pushed out. When the claws were out, they were deadly.

Claws that go in and out are "retractable." This helps protect the claws.

Saber-toothed cats also had strong, heavy bodies. Their neck and shoulder muscles were especially strong. They made it easy for the cats to pounce on an animal and hold it down.

Life in the Pack

The La Brea Tar Pits contained saber-toothed cats of all ages. Scientists discovered some animals had serious injuries. Many had hurt themselves before falling in the pit. Some showed signs of healing. But how did these injured animals care for themselves?

Bones of saber-toothed cats are often found together. Scientists believe they lived in groups. They think that healthy saber-toothed cats let injured ones eat part of their kills. This gave the injured animals time to heal.

Saber-Toothed Cats
Large canine teeth
Strong bodies
Pounced on victims
Lived in groups

How Did They Eat?

How did saber-toothed cats chew with those huge teeth? Researchers found the cats could open their jaws very wide . . . much wider than cats today.

Some scientists think saber-toothed cats bit meat off from the sides of their mouth. They had sharp teeth in the back of their mouth. They used these to shred the meat.

One wolf fossil had a piece of a saber-toothed cat's tooth stuck in its head!

We know saber-toothed cats prowled the earth millions of years ago. They became extinct about 11,000 years ago. Scientists don't know why this happened. Some think people hunted them too much. Others think they ran out of food when the climate changed.

Even though these cats disappeared long ago, the sticky asphalt at La Brea holds great clues about their lives.

Scientists Who Dig Up the Past

Archaeologists call the site they're working on a "dig."

Archaeologists (ar-kee-OL-uh-jists) are scientists who study ancient people. When they find an ancient campsite, they look for lots of things . . . tools, pieces of pottery, weapons, and human remains like bones. They carefully dig up what they've found. All these things give them clues about people of the past.

Paleontologists (pay-lee-un-TOL-uh-jists) are scientists who study early plant and animal life. They like to study ancient fossils of animals, insects, and plants. These things tell them what the world was like long ago . . . even before people existed!

Paleontologists and archaeologists work a lot alike. They go to sites and carefully dig up clues. They make drawings and take photographs. Then they record their information. They're like history detectives!

71

6

Mammoths in the Ice

Siberia is a vast, cold part of Russia. In 1977, a man operating a bulldozer made a discovery. As he worked, he saw a dark shape in the ice. He looked closer. He was amazed! He thought he'd found a baby elephant buried in the ice!

Scientists rushed to examine his find. The elephant was actually an extinct Ice Age animal called a woolly mammoth! It was about six months old when it died. Its body had been buried for thousands of years.

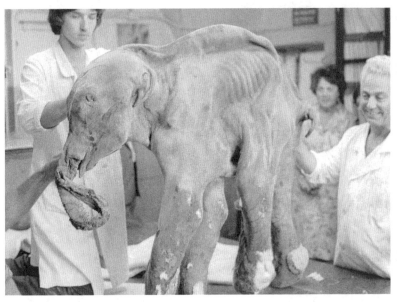

This baby mammoth lived 10,000 years ago!

Woolly Mammoths

Over 4,500 frozen mammoths have been discovered in Siberia. Mammoths belong to the elephant family. Finding their frozen bodies has helped scientists learn much about their lives.

Woolly mammoths lived in Siberia, Europe, and North America. The weather there was *frigid*.

Frigid means "really cold!"

Animals couldn't survive in that icebox without protection. Woolly mammoths were loaded with warm hair. It was long and shaggy . . . sometimes it was three feet long!

One woolly mammoth hair is as thick as six human hairs.

In addition, they had a layer of fat under their skin. The fat stored heat. When there was no food, fat gave them energy.

Woolly mammoths were usually about ten feet tall at the shoulder. They weighed over four tons. They had huge tusks. Males had longer tusks than females. Scientists have discovered tusks over 13 feet long. Mammoths used their tusks for defense against predators. Since they ate plants, they used their tusks to dig grasses and plants out of the snow.

These woolly mammoth tusks were found in Siberia.

Other Mammoths

Woolly mammoths were just one type of mammoth. Other types lived all over the world. Some were as tall as giraffes. Others were about as tall as a man.

The largest were the Columbian mammoths. They lived in North America. The males were over 13 feet tall at the shoulder and weighed over nine tons! The smallest were the pygmy mammoths. They were about six feet tall. They lived on islands off the coast of California.

Columbian

Woolly

Pygmy

In 1807, President Thomas Jefferson sent Captain William Clark on a mission. Clark was a great explorer. But this time his job was to bring back animal bones found in Kentucky. No one knew what kind of bones they were. The bones lay in a place called Big Bone Lick.

Jefferson and his friend Benjamin Franklin were puzzled. They decided the bones were elephant bones. Today we know they were mammoth bones. You can still see the bones in Jefferson's house in Virginia.

Mammoths like those at Big Bone Lick are called "Jefferson's mammoths."

Mammoth Families

Mammoths lived in herds. Males were part of the herd, but they often roamed about on their own. The female mammoths had to stick together. It was their job to care for the babies. Most mammoths had from five to 15 babies in their lifetime. Like modern elephants, the females looked after each other's babies as well as their own.

Scientists think females were the bosses of the herd.

Predators

Mammoths often had to fight off predators like people or saber-toothed cats. If danger was near, a mammoth trumpeted a note of alarm. They all moved in close together. The baby mammoths hid behind their mothers.

The adults used their sharp tusks to fight off the intruders. They also used their huge legs to stomp on their enemies.

Hunting a Mammoth

Remains of a mammoth were found on a ranch in Naco, Arizona. Its skeleton had eight spear points stuck in it!

Mammoth skin was thick and hard to stick with a spear.

Archaeologists think that humans killed mammoths in several different ways. One way was to attack them with spears.

Another method was to set fires around the herds. The frightened animals raced off high cliffs trying to escape. They often died in the fall. If they didn't, the hunters killed them at the bottom of the cliff.

There are about eight sites that show evidence of mammoth hunting.

Scientists have also found large holes with mammoth remains in them. They think the hunters dug holes. Then they covered them with branches. The mammoths fell into the holes. The hunters threw heavy stones down on the animals

82

to kill them. Then they speared the ones left alive.

Scientists don't think hunting caused the mammoths to become totally extinct. But they think it played a big part.

Turn the page to meet more of our favorite Ice Age animals!

Woolly Rhino

In Britain, a woolly rhino was dug up with a plant stuck in its teeth.

Woolly rhinos became extinct about 20,000 years ago. Their fossils have turned up from Britain to Siberia. Scientists have studied the actual body of a woolly rhino. They found it buried in mud in the Ukraine.

Woolly rhinos ate grass. They lived in herds. Their long, shaggy coats protected them from the cold. The rhinos measured about six feet tall at the shoulder. Many were over 11 feet long and weighed more than a car! They also had two large horns above their noses. The horns were made of thick, strong hair. They were useful for fighting. They were also good for digging up food like grasses and plants buried in the snow.

Giant Ground Sloth

Giant ground sloths lived in North and South America. They were very strange animals. These sloths were as big as elephants. They weighed three to four tons. And that's not all! Standing upright, they were as tall as a giraffe!

Scientists think giant ground sloths sometimes walked upright.

The sloth had incredible claws. They were as big as a man's arm. Fortunately these gigantic animals didn't eat people. They ate plants and fruit. Like modern sloths, they moved very, very slowly. Giant ground sloths became extinct about 12,000 years ago.

Cave Lion

Modern lions are a little over eight feet long.

There are cave paintings and fossils of huge lions. They lived in caves in Europe. These lions were over 11 feet long. That's much bigger than lions today. But like lions today, they were meat-eaters.

Carvings and cave paintings exist of creatures who were half man, half lion. Archaeologists think that early people thought these lions had magic power. Maybe the artists thought they could have the power of a lion. Cave lions lasted a long time. The last ones disappeared only 2,000 years ago.

Cave Bear

Like cave lions, cave bears made their homes in caves. Some caves have thousands of their skeletons. In a cave in France, there are huge bear footprints. In many caves, marks from bear claws are all over the walls.

Cave bears were about ten feet tall! One skin would make a whole tent! But these huge creatures didn't eat meat. They were vegetarians.

Archaeologists think Ice Age people used cave bear skulls and teeth for ceremonies. One German cave had ten bear skulls on a ledge. In the same cave, scientists found 310 bear teeth.

Glyptodont

Glyptodonts (GLIP-tuh-donts) are like nothing you've ever seen! At first, scientists could not even figure out what they were.

These strange creatures lived in North America. They were almost five feet tall and over nine feet long. By looking at fossils, scientists have guessed that bony scales covered their bodies and foreheads. The scales acted like armor. There were little holes in the scales. Hairs sprouted out of the holes.

Only part of the glyptodonts' faces and legs were not protected.

Glyptodonts were vegetarians. They lived on grasslands or near water. Imagine seeing an animal the size of a car munching away on your front yard!

Giant Beaver

There are ancient Indian stories about giant beavers. Fossils tell us these beavers actually existed. They lived near lakes and swamps in North America. They were the biggest *rodents* that ever lived. Many weighed over 400 pounds. (A modern beaver weighs about 65 pounds.)

Rodents are animals like rats and mice that have special teeth for gnawing.

And they were about eight feet tall when they stood up. That's the size of a black bear!

We don't know exactly what the giant beavers looked like. Scientists guess they looked a lot like beavers today . . . only much bigger!

Dire Wolf

The Ice Age dire wolves were larger than wolves today. They were about five feet long and weighed more than 110 pounds. They had strong legs and a wide head.

The dire wolves seemed to have hunted in packs. They had extremely large, powerful teeth. Scientists think they used them to crush the bones of their prey. Their teeth could also grip large animals and hang on tightly.

More than 3,600 dire wolves have been found in the La Brea Tar Pits. Many of their skulls show signs of injury. Scientists think they got these wounds from being kicked in the head by animals they were attacking.

Western Camel

We usually think of camels living in deserts. Not these camels! They lived in the grasslands of North America 50 million years ago. They lived on into the Ice Age.

Western camels were about seven feet tall at the shoulder. Scientists think they had a single hump on their backs. They ate plants.

Scientists discovered camel bones with cut marks on them. The marks were made by early Native Americans. Experts wonder if the Native Americans ate camel burgers for dinner!

Here's another interesting fact about Western camels. Along with horses and some other animals, they were among the few animals that traveled the land bridge from North America into Asia and Africa. Most animals traveled the opposite way.

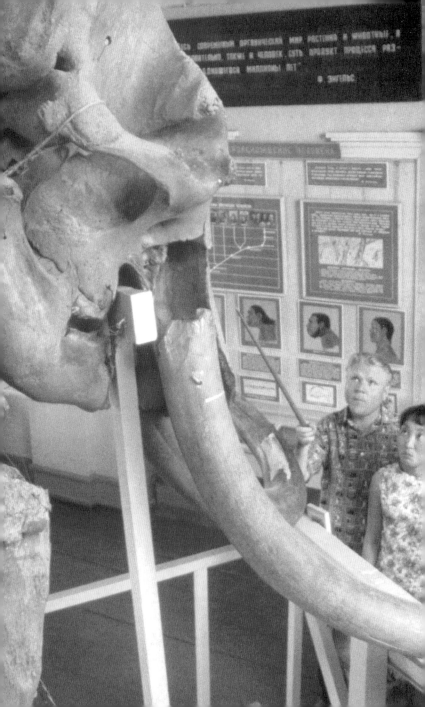

7

After the Ice Age

The Ice Age came to an end about 10,000 years ago. Earth's orbit moved closer to the sun. The world began to get warmer. Much of the ice began to melt. Ocean levels rose. The land bridges disappeared.

Many animals became extinct. Scientists don't know why the animals disappeared.

But they do have several *theories* (THEER-eez). Theories are ideas that haven't been proved.

One theory is that when the weather changed, some plants died off. Animals began to run out of food. Another idea is that a terrible disease wiped out the animals. A third idea is that too much hunting caused their extinction.

Scientists are still looking for clues. One thing they're doing is studying mammoth tusks. The tusks show if the animal was sick when it died. They also show what time of the year it died. This study may provide clues as to why mammoths became extinct.

Other Ice Age animals exist today. By studying them, we can understand their ancient relatives. Moose still exist. Grizzly bears and bison survived. Another animal also may have survived. It is a type of Ice Age dog. These wild dogs

People have kept dogs as pets for over 14,000 years!

live in the woods of South Carolina. Some
researchers think they could be relatives
of dogs from the Ice Age.

Moose

Grizzly bears

Bison

The climate change also affected the people of the Ice Age. As the climate warmed up, people stopped following the great herds. The warmer weather made it easier to plant crops. Villages sprang up around farms. Villages grew into cities.

The population also grew. At the end of the Ice Age, there were about five million people in the whole world. That's less than the population of New York City today!

Population means "the number of people that live in one place."

Our Ice Age ancestors lived in a harsh world. Experts think they survived by helping one another. They hunted together. They shared food and cared for the sick and the old. And they did more than just survive. They created beautiful art that inspires us today.

The people and great animals of the Ice Age still fill us with awe. Imagine creeping into a cave 15,000 years ago. It is icy cold and snowing. You need to warm up. Suddenly something in the back of the cave moves. It is huge. Outside the wind is howling. Slowly and carefully you back out of the entrance. Inside the cave, a giant cave bear stirs. Then he sighs and turns over for a good winter's sleep.

Doing More Research

There's a lot more you can learn about sabertooths and the Ice Age. The fun of research is seeing how many different sources you can explore.

Books

Most libraries and bookstores have books about sabertooths and the Ice Age.

Here are some things to remember when you're using books for research:

1. You don't have to read the whole book. Check the table of contents and the index to find the topics you're interested in.

2. Write down the name of the book.
When you take notes, make sure you write down the name of the book in your notebook so you can find it again.

3. Never copy exactly from a book.
When you learn something new from a book, put it in your own words.

4. Make sure the book is <u>nonfiction</u>.
Some books tell make-believe stories about sabertooths and the Ice Age. Make-believe stories are called *fiction*. They're fun to read, but not good for research.

Research books have facts and tell true stories. They are called *nonfiction*. A librarian or teacher can help you make sure the books you use for research are nonfiction.

Here are some good nonfiction books about sabertooths and the Ice Age:

- *Cave Detectives: Unraveling the Mystery of an Ice Age Cave* by David L. Harrison

- *Early Humans*, a DK Eyewitness Book

- *Ice Age Mammals of North America: A Guide to the Big, the Hairy, and the Bizarre* by Ian M. Lange

- *Ice Age Sabertooth: The Most Ferocious Cat that Ever Lived* by Barbara Hehner

- *The Ice Age Tracker's Guide* by Adrian Lister

- *Mammoths and Mastodons: Titans of the Ice Age* by Cheryl Bardoe

Museums

Many museums have Ice Age exhibits. You can also visit some sites where fossils have been found! These places can help you learn more about sabertooths and the Ice Age.

When you go to a museum:

1. Be sure to take your notebook!
Write down anything that catches your interest. Draw pictures, too!

2. Ask questions.
There are almost always people at museums who can help you find what you're looking for.

3. Check the calendar.
Many museums have special events and activities just for kids!

Here are some museums with exhibits about the Ice Age:

- American Museum of Natural History (New York)

- Big Bone Lick State Park (Union, Kentucky)

- Burke Museum of Natural History and Culture (Seattle)

- Denver Museum of Nature and Science

- The Mammoth Site (Hot Springs, South Dakota)

- Page Museum at the La Brea Tar Pits (Los Angeles)

DVDs

There are some great nonfiction DVDs about the Ice Age. As with books, make sure the DVDs you watch for research are nonfiction!

Check your library or video store for these and other nonfiction titles about the Ice Age:

- *Baby Mammoth*
  from Discovery Channel

- *Glaciers*
  from Ambrose Video

- *Mammoth Mystery*
  from National Geographic

- *Prehistoric Predators: Sabertooth*
  from National Geographic

The Internet

Many websites have facts about the Ice Age. Some also have games and activities that can help make learning about the Ice Age even more fun.

Ask your teacher or your parents to help you find more websites like these:

- bbc.co.uk/nature/life/Mammal/by/prehistoric

- crystalinks.com/woollyrhino.html

- dmns.org/main/minisites/iceage/index.html

- enchantedlearning.com/subjects/mammals/Iceagemammals.shtml

- highlightskids.com/Science/Stories/SS0199_droppingsofmammoth.asp

- kids.nationalgeographic.com/kids/animals
  /creaturefeature/mammoths

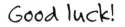

Index

117

Have you read the adventure that matches up with this book?

Don't miss

Magic Tree House® #7

SUNSET OF THE SABERTOOTH

Jack and Annie nearly freeze when the magic tree house whisks them back to the time of cave people and woolly mammoths. But nothing can stop them from having another wild adventure—not even a sabertooth!

Magic Tree House®

Magic Tree House® Merlin Missions

Magic Tree House®
Super Edition

#1: WORLD AT WAR, 1944

Magic Tree House®
Fact Trackers

DINOSAURS

KNIGHTS AND CASTLES

MUMMIES AND PYRAMIDS

PIRATES

RAIN FORESTS

SPACE

TITANIC

TWISTERS AND OTHER TERRIBLE STORMS

DOLPHINS AND SHARKS

ANCIENT GREECE AND THE OLYMPICS

AMERICAN REVOLUTION

SABERTOOTHS AND THE ICE AGE

PILGRIMS

ANCIENT ROME AND POMPEII

TSUNAMIS AND OTHER NATURAL DISASTERS

POLAR BEARS AND THE ARCTIC

SEA MONSTERS

PENGUINS AND ANTARCTICA

LEONARDO DA VINCI

GHOSTS

LEPRECHAUNS AND IRISH FOLKLORE

RAGS AND RICHES: KIDS IN THE TIME OF
    CHARLES DICKENS

SNAKES AND OTHER REPTILES

DOG HEROES

ABRAHAM LINCOLN

PANDAS AND OTHER ENDANGERED SPECIES

HORSE HEROES

HEROES FOR ALL TIMES

SOCCER

NINJAS AND SAMURAI

CHINA: LAND OF THE EMPEROR'S GREAT
    WALL

SHARKS AND OTHER PREDATORS

VIKINGS

DOGSLEDDING AND EXTREME SPORTS

DRAGONS AND MYTHICAL CREATURES

WORLD WAR II

More Magic Tree House®

GAMES AND PUZZLES FROM THE TREE HOUSE

MAGIC TRICKS FROM THE TREE HOUSE

MY MAGIC TREE HOUSE JOURNAL

MAGIC TREE HOUSE SURVIVAL GUIDE

ANIMAL GAMES AND PUZZLES

MAGIC TREE HOUSE INCREDIBLE FACT BOOK